Your Amazing Itty Bitty™ End the Pity Party Now!

15 Ways to Leave the Past and Step Into Your Future

Keri A. Bentsen

Published by Itty Bitty™ Publishing
A subsidiary of S & P Productions, Inc.

Copyright © 2025 Keri A. Bentsen

All rights reserved. No part of this book may be reproduced or transmitted in any form or by any means, electronic or mechanical, including photocopying, recording, or by any information storage and retrieval system, without written permission of the publisher, except for the inclusion of brief quotations in a review.

Printed in the United States of America

Itty Bitty Publishing
311 Main Street, Suite D
El Segundo, CA 90245
(310) 640-8885

ISBN: 978-1-959964-78-0

This book is for educational purposes only. Nothing should be taken as mental health advice, diagnosis or treatment. Always seek the guidance of a mental health professional should you need assistance.

Are you feeling stuck in your story? Tired of the pity party that never seems to end?

Here are 15 Ways to Leave the Past and Step Into Your Future

Life throws curveballs, and when things feel unfair, it's easy to give in to self-pity. But staying stuck won't get you anywhere. Telling yourself to get over it just doesn't work. You may try to numb the pain and feelings with food, bingeing on TV, alcohol or distractions, but the feelings always come back stronger, and you're even more miserable.

In her powerful book, *Your Amazing Itty Bitty™ End the Pity Party Now*, transformational coach Keri A. Bentsen provides you with the action steps to offer yourself compassion and permission to move through each phase with love and grace. She will show you how to leave the past behind and step into the future version of yourself.

Keri will show you how to:

- Look for solutions
- Learn from your missteps
- Create a mindset that moves you forward
- Show up as your future self, starting now

If you're ready to end the "Pity Party" of your life and move on to a brighter future, pick up a copy of this must-read Itty Bitty™ book today!

Dedication

This book is dedicated to you, a human who has dealt with disappointments in life and wants to stop feeling bad about yourself.

Let's face it, when others tell you or you tell yourself to "get over it," it just doesn't work. So, you suppress your feelings and do surface things you don't have to think much about to mask your feelings about yourself. You binge on food or binge-watch Netflix and end up at a full-blown pity party. Then you feel a little better, until the same pattern sneaks back in again on repeat.

Let's end the pity party now!

In this book, you will find healthy ways to break that cycle. You'll learn how to unpack what you're feeling and walk through it step by step, to finally leave the past behind and become the future version of yourself you've been longing to meet.

There are also free resources on my website to help guide you through each phase of your pity party. You can check them out here: https://endpitypartybook.com

You've got this! Let the (transformational) pity party begin so you can end it for good!

Stop by our Itty Bitty™ website to find interesting information regarding
End the Pity Party Now:
15 Steps to Leave the Past and Step Into Your Future

www.IttyBittyPublishing.com

Or visit Keri Bentsen at

http://KeriBentsen.com

Table of Contents

Introduction
- Step 1. Why a Pity Party?
- Step 2. Hosting a Transformative Pity Party
- Step 3. Preparations for Your Party
- Step 4. Your Guest List
- Step 5. Plan Your Menu
- Step 6. Select Your Music
- Step 7. Deconstruct and Redecorate Your Space
- Step 8. It's Time to Clean Up the Mess
- Step 9. Before You End the Party
- Step 10. Put New Habits in Place
- Step 11. Time to Open Your Gifts!
- Step 12. Thank You Notes
- Step 13. Leave Your Past Behind: Forgiveness
- Step 14. Keep Moving Forward; Set Daily Intentions
- Step 15. Step Into Your Future

Introduction

Life is full of ups and downs. When it feels unfair, it's natural to give in to self-pity. However, it's important not to stay there.

Although this book uses the word *party* as a pun, I'm not making fun of the process. Rather, it's an invitation for you, the reader, to offer yourself compassion and give yourself permission to move through each phase with love and grace. This will support your healing process, help you release your past, and allow you to process your emotions so you can move toward your future self with a renewed mindset.

This book outlines action steps to have a *transformative* pity party that walks you through 15 powerful phases to help you leave the past and step into your future.

There is no right way to go through this process. I recommend reading the book and deciding for yourself which steps resonate most. Pick and choose what feels right to you. The important thing is to begin so you can move forward in peace and finally leave the past behind for good.

Step 1
Why a Pity Party?

Before deciding to end your pity party, it's helpful to understand why you're having one; otherwise, you might find yourself unintentionally having another one down the road.

Some common reasons may include:

1. Burnout and exhaustion; feeling overwhelmed with life.
2. Feeling unappreciated: "Woe is me."
3. Feeling stuck in negative emotions: "I'm not good enough."
4. Repeated setbacks: "Life isn't fair."
5. Unmet expectations: "Why me?"

Here are some signs that the pity party has overstayed its welcome:

1. You keep replaying the same sad story.
2. You blame everyone else for your problems.
3. You lack motivation to try new things.
4. You constantly complain without changing.
5. You withdraw from others.
6. You feel resentment towards others' success, or feel bitter or jealous.

More About Reasons for Your Pity Party

Initially, pity parties are "feel-good" coping mechanisms when you face challenges. However, you can feel stuck if you:

- Stop looking for solutions
- Do nothing to change the situation
- Avoid hearing advice or encouragement
- Find it easier to stay where you are
- Lack motivation to move ahead

Staying in that mindset is not only unproductive but also damaging to your mental health. Here are some ways to counteract those feelings:

- Realize that you're not the only one feeling this way. Generally, you see others at their best while seeing yourself at your worst.
- Social media and real-life comparisons can make you feel like you're falling behind.
- Other people's lives usually look easier, but chances are, they are going through their own challenges.
- When someone is successful, you don't see the struggles they faced.
- Sitting in pity sometimes feels easier than taking action to change a difficult situation.

Step 2
Hosting a Transformative Pity Party

You're done with self-pity because you know it doesn't serve you. Good for you!

1. You're tired of living this way and want to feel better.
2. You're ready to move on and say goodbye to your old self.
3. It's time to welcome and step into your future self.

Plan your transformative pity party, a process to intentionally shift your focus from repeating negative spirals of self-doubt and hopelessness, to take positive action that improves your outlook on life. This includes:

1. Feeling and processing your emotions
2. Observing your thoughts
3. Knowing the difference between a fact and a story you tell yourself
4. Learning what your triggers are
5. Graduating from self-judgment to self-compassion
6. Self-reflection and journaling
7. Practicing gratitude
8. Forgiving yourself and others

More on Hosting a Transformative Pity Party

Implement "Yhprum's" law, where whatever can work, will work, as opposed to Murphy's Law, which says whatever can go wrong, will go wrong. "Yhprum" is Murphy spelled backward.

- Look for solutions rather than problems.
- Learn from failures, which are just feedback for what didn't work.
- Adopt a growth mindset, rather than a fixed mindset.

This is comparable to the Law of Attraction, where like attracts like. Practice and be in positive energy to attract more positivity.

- Set the intention that things will work out.
- Visualize success: Picture how you want your life to look, and make a plan for it to happen.
- Start with the end in mind and work your way backwards.
- Act as if what you want will work out in the end.
- Expect the outcome you want, or something better.
- Imagine what it would feel like to have that life and sit with those feelings.
- Be grateful for what you have right now. Gratitude attracts more positive experiences in your life.

Step 3
Preparations for Your Party

Yes, you're planning your last pity party! The sooner the better, like tomorrow or next weekend. Here's what you need to do:

1. Select a date on your calendar.
2. It can be for a few hours or an entire day. Longer is not recommended.
3. Block out this time and make sure nothing gets booked or in the way of this event. Mark yourself as unavailable.
4. Let your family and friends know that you're busy and unavailable.
5. Minimize distractions. Turn off notifications.

This might feel a little scary and exciting at the same time.

1. It's crucial to be mentally and emotionally ready for this experience.
2. Avoid the temptation to procrastinate and postpone the party.
3. If you're reading this book, you're ready.
4. Your future self is waiting for you.

More on Preparations for Your Party

You're declaring goodbye to the old and making room for the new. This step requires adopting new beliefs.

- Change is hard; so is staying where you are. Choose the hard one you want to implement.
- "Change takes but an instant; it's the resistance to change that takes the time." ~ *Canyon Ranch*
- Change your attitude. Smile about the future, banish frowns from the past.

Studies show that humans have between 6,000-60,000 thoughts per day, many of which are repetitive and negative. Break free from limiting beliefs tied to your past to step into a more authentic and uplifting version of yourself.

- From "everything always goes wrong for me," to "I acknowledge I've faced challenges, but I'm not defined by them. I have strength to overcome obstacles."
- From "I'm stuck and there's no way out," to "I can create positive change in my life. I may need to take small steps, but I am moving forward."
- From "I'm not strong enough to handle this," to "I'm stronger than I think. I'm discovering my inner strength and resilience."

Step 4
Your Guest List

Your guests are all the emotions and feelings surrounding your self-pity. Make a list of each attitude as if each were a person. For example:

1. Vinny Victim
2. Ronny Resentment
3. Woeful Wendy
4. Hopeless Harry
5. Faultless Frank
6. Angry Angela
7. Shameful Sam
8. Misfortune Mandy

Now, make another list of impactful guests you want in your life to replace the self-pity guests. You will need these people to act as your support system and encourage growth. For example:

1. Merry Melissa
2. Grateful Gary
3. Compassionate Carrie
4. Joyful Judy
5. Resilient Randy
6. Felicia Faithful
7. Determined Dave
8. Forgiving Felix

More About Your Guest List

Emotions and feelings are neutral, so try not to put them in good or bad categories. Don't be so quick to judge them and stuff them in a box, because each time you do, they come back to you. They need to be dealt with properly so they can go away for good.

- Journal about each of your guests (feelings) and be curious about them.
- Investigate and learn all you can about each one and validate them.
- Be curious about your triggers, and decide how you want to react to them moving forward. Make a plan.

Once you have processed and given each guest the attention they've been yearning for, it's time to let them go.

- Hold each one in your thoughts and thank them for the time they spent with you.
- Forgive them for any harm they have caused in your life. This frees you.
- When you feel ready, say good-bye and tell them you don't need them anymore.
- Wish them well and tell them you're going to be fine from now on.
- Breathe a sigh of relief as you let each one go.
- Have faith that you're going to be okay without them.

Step 5
Plan Your Menu

What you feed yourself physically and emotionally affects how you feel. It's time to clear out your pantry and refuel with positivity.

1. Make a list of the comfort foods that soothe but leave you feeling sluggish.
2. Physically take those foods out and put them on your counter.
3. Look at the nutrients. Educate yourself about what's in the food you eat.

These foods often parallel your emotional state. Are those foods keeping you stuck in a cycle of bitterness?

1. Do these foods nourish you or drain you?
2. Analyze what's best for your body and mind.
3. Decide to stop feeding your pity with food that makes you feel blah.
4. When you're ready, make a conscious decision to remove those foods from your home.
5. Don't think of this as "have to." Find valid reasons that feel good to you.
6. Decide now which foods you want to replace them with.

More on Planning Your Menu

Clean out your refrigerator and your freezer as well.

- Make a list of foods you love that are packed with nutrition.
- Choose foods that make you feel strong and energized.
- Eating well is an act of self-care.
- You deserve delicious food that makes you feel good inside.
- Trade in mindless emotional snacking for intentional nourishment.

Your body isn't the only thing that needs nourishment; your mind does, too. Reset your emotional nutrition and fill yourself with gratitude. Serve yourself a healthy dose of self-compassion every day.

- Change your menu, and you'll change your mindset.
- Do an internet search or go to your local library for personal development books to fuel your mind with new knowledge and spark new ideas for your life.
- Find a new hobby or restart an old one you used to enjoy. This adds fun back into your life and gives your mind something new to think about.
- Plan a weekend getaway or a vacation to have something for you to look forward to.

Step 6
Select Your Music

Let's face it, when you hear an old familiar song, it evokes a memory or feeling inside you.

1. Music activates the limbic system. This is the part of the brain that controls emotion and memory.
2. Certain songs and lyrics may be tied to periods in your life or relationships that trigger strong memories and emotions when you hear them.
3. Music releases dopamine; it can lift your mood and help regulate emotions.
4. Sing or hum along to songs that remind you of the past. Allow yourself to express your emotions (crying, yelling) to release those pent-up feelings.

Shift your mindset about those songs to help you move on.

1. Allow yourself to feel your emotions to help process your thoughts.
2. Be mindful of when to stop to avoid getting stuck in a cycle of sadness. If necessary, set a timer.
3. Journal your thoughts. Read what you have written as an observer and categorize it as a season in your life.

More About Selecting Your Music

Chances are, you will likely hear this music or song again in your future.

- Allow the thought, "I remember those days," and apply a different but positive mental label to it.
- Reminisce with a different perspective. "Those days taught me life lessons, and I wouldn't be here today if I hadn't gone through that period." Or use something more fitting for your situation.

Create a "moving on" Playlist. Music is a bridge from sadness to healing and allows you to move from feeling stuck to looking forward to your future.

- Upbeat music boosts energy. Fast tempos and positive lyrics can reinforce self-worth, adaptability, and confidence.
- Happy music releases serotonin.
- Sing and dance! Engage with music physically to help you feel lighter and break emotional stagnation.
- Start a daily exercise habit and play your favorite music genre.
- Use music as a daily mood booster. Playing background music as you work can improve your mood and boost your productivity.

Step 7
Deconstruct and Redecorate Your Space

Look around your home. Are there memories hanging on your walls or on the refrigerator? Does it make you sad every time you see it? If so, it might be time to remove those things from sight. Get ready with two boxes: donate and storage.

1. Go through each room of your home. Collect items tied to your outdated identity, and replace those that may no longer serve your future self.
2. Ask yourself if you value that item more than you value your future identity.
3. Decide what to do with each item.

You might feel a need to hang onto certain items for sentimental reasons or fear of change. Things often carry some emotional weight. Sit with those thoughts and journal about them. Then ask yourself these questions:

1. Do I want to see this item in my home every day?
2. What feelings will this item evoke in me every time I look at it?
3. Can someone else benefit from this item?
4. If you're not sure about certain items, put them in storage and decide on them later.

More About Deconstruct and Redecorate Your Space

Now the fun begins! When your home is free of items from your past that no longer serve you, it's time to redecorate your space. Here are some inexpensive ways to give your home a welcoming refresh.

- Declutter and organize what's left.
- Do a deep clean of the carpet, furniture, and surroundings.
- Plan a time to give your walls a fresh coat of paint or design an accent wall.
- Rearrange the furniture in a fun, inviting way.

Sometimes the best way to shift your feelings is to change your surroundings. Small changes can have a huge impact on your psyche. Think of how you want your space to feel when you come home. Here are some more creative ideas to uplevel your space.

- Add bright pops of color with accent pillows.
- Bring nature inside with plants.
- Hang artwork or photos that represent who you are now.
- Create a vision board and display it.
- Upgrade your curtains or blinds and let the sunshine in.
- Add string lights or a small lamp to create a warm, welcoming vibe.

Step 8
It's Time to Clean Up the Mess

Good job! You've tackled the physical clutter from your past. Now it's time to address the mental mess that has been weighing you down.

1. Sweep out negative thoughts about the past. They will pop up, so it's important to be aware of them and not judge them.
2. Challenge those thoughts. Are they true? Is each thought helping or hurting me?
3. Name the story you're telling yourself. This separates you from the story and allows you to see it as just that: a story.
4. Do a brain dump, where you journal on what's in your head. This allows you to see patterns, organize your thoughts, and release mental clutter.

When you notice yourself spiraling or having negative thoughts, say "Stop!" out loud or in your mind, then continue with the following tips.

1. Allow yourself compassion.
2. Speak kindly as you would to someone you love.
3. Change your scenery or something else to distract yourself.
4. Realize that harsh thoughts don't lead to growth, but kindness does.

More About Clean Up the Mess

Clearing your mind of self-criticism and doubt takes practice. An effective strategy is using positive reframing.

- Instead of, "I always mess things up," try "I've learned a lot, and I'm making better choices now."
- Instead of, "I'm not good enough," try "I am capable and worthy, and I'm learning and growing every day."
- Instead of, "I'm overweight, and no one is interested in me," try "I'm worthy just as I am, and being authentic is more appealing than trying to fit into someone else's ideal."

Don't wait until you have it all figured out to acknowledge how far you've come. Remember, you're not trying to erase your past; you're just choosing not to live there anymore.

- Keep journaling: it's a powerful tool for self-discovery, emotional well-being, and personal growth.
- Surround yourself with positivity, be it with people, news, social media, etc. Choose input that uplifts and inspires without draining you.
- Celebrate progress, not perfection. Persistence is key to success.
- Keep moving forward, no matter what.

Step 9
Before You End the Party

Before you move forward, it's helpful to ground yourself where you are right now, which means being mindful.

1. Focus on the present moment, in the here and now; not what has happened in the past or what might be in the future.
2. Let go of the "what ifs" and the "I should have" from the past. They will only keep you stuck.
3. The more present you are, the less power your past has over you.

Focus on what's real right now using your senses.

1. Become aware of what you're thinking and feeling right now with no judgment.
2. Notice what's happening in front of you where you are. Are you fully aware of your senses?
3. Pay attention to what you see with your eyes. Appreciate the beautiful colors.
4. What do you hear when you really listen?
5. What do you smell? Take it all in.
6. When you eat, do you savor every bite?
7. When you pet your dog or cat, or hug someone, do you take in the feeling?

More About Before You End Your Party

Leaving a pity party isn't just feeling better; it's also you choosing where you're headed next. This is an opportunity for you to map out your future.

- Write out what you truly want, without limits.
- Break down your big goals into small, action steps.
- Shift your attention to what's ahead, not stuck wishing how to change the past.

Moving on means things will change, and that can be scary. Change can be exciting and uncomfortable at the same time. Your new path is trading pain for possibility. Being in the present moment, vision and change are tools you will need to move forward and close down the pity party once and for all.

- Staying where you are because it's familiar won't get you what you want.
- Choosing to let go of the familiar so you can grow is a sign of trusting yourself, despite uncertainty
- Choosing faith over fear is a declaration to help you progress and strengthen your mental muscle

For more on this, download my free Mindfulness Checklist and Guided Journal here: https://free.wellnesstweaks.com/

Step 10
Put New Habits in Place

First, decide which habits you want to get rid of, which new ones you want to implement, and then write them down. To avoid overwhelm, try not to start a lot of new habits at once. The following are some tips to guide you.

1. Understand what triggers your current (undesired) habit. Then start by phasing out one old habit and replacing it with a new one that benefits you more.
2. Make old habits unpleasant and inconvenient. Find valid reasons to avoid them. Make new habits easy and fun.
3. Start small and work your way up. If you want to get up an hour earlier, start by getting up 10 minutes earlier (and going to bed 10 minutes earlier) and gradually work your way up to an hour.
4. Avoid all-or-nothing thinking. Aim for 80% progress, not 100% perfection.
5. Stay connected to your "why." Remind yourself why this is important to you and stay motivated.
6. Celebrate small wins. At the end of the day, think about how things went and commend yourself for what you accomplished, rather than what you didn't.

More About Putting New Habits in Place

Studies show that although it takes 21 days to form a new habit, it can take around 90 days for it to become a lifestyle. It's important to be patient and keep going no matter what. Here are some tips:

- Surround yourself with supportive people or a partner to keep you accountable.
- Don't judge or shame yourself if you slip. You're human; give yourself grace and compassion.
- Anchor a new habit by tying it to a current one (from *Atomic Habits* by James Clear). If you want to start flossing, put the floss next to your toothbrush so you can get in the habit of using them together
- Set up for success: put your gym clothes by the door or in your car the night before.
- Visualize the life you're creating. Picture yourself living the new version of your life.

This chapter is your turning point. When the right habits are in place, you'll no longer react to life; you'll create the one you want. Keep showing up to make the biggest long-term impact to support who you're becoming. You're not just changing habits, you're changing your story.

Step 11
Time to Open Your Gifts!

You've done the work. You cleaned up the mental mess and your physical space. It's time to unwrap all the gifts that have formed while you were healing. These gifts are the strengths and inner tools you've gained by staying on course and choosing not to stay stuck.

1. Self-Awareness: You are now in touch with your thoughts, patterns and triggers.
2. Emotional Strength: You've survived tough times and now can face anything.
3. Confidence: By moving forward, you are more capable than you thought.
4. Peace of Mind: Letting go of the past creates space for new possibilities.

These aren't presents someone else gives you. You didn't ask for the struggle, but you've earned those gifts from your trials and triumphs.

1. Clarity: Your past experiences have equipped you with better perception and understanding, enabling you to make better decisions from here on.
2. Appreciation: You gain a deeper sense of self, purpose, and increased capacity for empathy.

More About Time to Open Your Gifts!

You are strong! You could have stayed where it's comfortable and held onto the pain that kept you stuck in the pity-party cycle, but you persevered. Past experiences that made you feel broken have built newfound strength you didn't know you had. You're not the same person; you've grown. As a result, these bonus gifts will keep on giving and enriching your life for years to come.

- Resilience: You have the capacity to withstand and bounce back from difficulties, and you've learned coping skills.
- Healthy boundaries: Saying no to staying stuck in the past means yes to your future self.
- Wisdom: Use your experience and knowledge to make sound judgments and decisions.

These gifts are yours to keep. Use them and trust them. They're living proof that your past doesn't define you; your growth does.

Step 12
Thank You Notes

Gratitude is like sending out thank you notes, not just to people, but to life itself. Here's a list of what you might be thankful for after ending your pity party.

1. Lessons learned from past mistakes show you've gained wisdom and growth.
2. Resilience is the strength you didn't know you had when you showed up for yourself.
3. Realizations of clarity are times when something clicked and you saw things differently.

Sending actual thank you notes to people who supported you can feel gratifying, including:

1. Friends who checked in on you.
2. Family who were there when you needed them most.
3. Loved ones who let you cry on their shoulder.
4. People who are no longer a part of your life, send a note listing what you're thankful for. You don't have to send it if you don't want to. Simply writing it can evoke appreciation.

More About Thank You Notes

When you end the pity party and choose to live with intention, you start seeing life through a different lens.

- The things that once made you cry are now better understood.
- You have a fresh perspective about what really matters; you no longer sweat the small stuff.
- Your pain has softened; you now realize the reason for what you went through.
- New healthy habits help you feel better every day.
- You've cleared out the old to make room for the new.
- Your newly refreshed space feels brand new.
- Your ability to forgive yourself and others leaves space to breathe and fills it with gratitude.
- You have the gift of starting over because you chose to end the pity party.

Gratitude closes this chapter with grace. It's your way of saying, "Thank you for my growth. I'm ready for what's next." So, take a moment to acknowledge not just the good times, but also the experiences that brought you here. The more you practice gratitude, the more it multiplies.

Step 13
Leave Your Past Behind: Forgiveness

Strong emotions like anger and resentment can create emotional attachment to past hurt, making it hard to move forward. Leaving the past behind doesn't mean pretending it didn't happen. You have a choice. You can choose not to carry that ball and chain anymore. You can make peace with your past with forgiveness:

1. People who unintentionally hurt you
2. Someone you trusted betrayed you
3. Others who disrespected you
4. Conflicts and disagreements with loved ones
5. Broken promises
6. Mistakes and errors in judgement
7. Anger at others who didn't show up the way you needed

Forgiveness is a personal process and doesn't always lead to reconciling with the person who hurt you, especially if trauma is involved.

1. Forgiving others doesn't mean you are letting them off the hook.
2. You free yourself from bondage.
3. Someone else's behavior is about them, not you.

More About Leaving Your Past Behind: Forgiveness

Perhaps the only thing that's harder than forgiving others for their wrongdoings is forgiving yourself. It's time to stop the following:

- Guilt and shame over past decisions
- Beating yourself up for not being perfect
- Regrets over missed chances or lost time
- Self-blame for things beyond your control
- Feeling of being stuck in the same old story

Forgiving yourself for what you didn't know, didn't do, or couldn't change, is an act of self-compassion to help you continue with greater insight. Decide to use today wisely instead of mourning yesterday. It's time to write a new story.

- I'm no longer who I used to be.
- I am a victor, not a victim.
- My past shaped me, but it doesn't define me.
- I don't need closure from others to move forward in peace.
- I forgive myself for how I coped while I was hurting.
- I deserve joy, healing, and a life that feels good from the inside out.

Step 14
Keep Moving Forward; Set Daily Intentions

You've done the hard work and made peace with your past. Congratulations! That's a huge accomplishment. Take a moment to accept this new reality and embrace it. Now, it's time to continue the process, to step into your future. This does ***not*** mean you have to have it all figured out. This means you keep pressing on. Here's how.

1. No more circling back to what was. Old habits will try to pull you back in. Don't let it happen; be strong!
2. Start walking in the new direction you want to go. Don't overthink it.
3. Stay grounded and focused on the present moment.

Sometimes, starting a new life chapter can feel scary and uncomfortable; however, it's important to keep advancing. It's okay to be afraid and do it anyway.

1. This is just your brain trying to protect you from danger of the unknown.
2. This is normal; however, don't give in! You will need to be brave and build that mental muscle to keep growing.

More About Keep Moving Forward to Set Daily Intentions

Stay on track by setting daily objectives that point you in the direction of your purpose. Intentions are powerful because they give purpose to get you started on your goals. Instead of letting the day control you, choose how you want to show up. Think of them as to-be lists, not to-do lists.

- Start your day by asking, "Who do I want to be today?"
- Write down one-to-three goals each morning.

Your future self is not an imaginary dream to have it all together one day. The small moments of lived experiences create your new being day after day.

- Visualize your future self and ask, "What should I do today?"
- Stay curious instead of critical. If you mess up, explore it rather than beat yourself up over it.
- Value progress, not perfection. Honor yourself for showing up and not giving up.
- When you live your intentions, you create new neural pathways in your brain.
- You build self-trust when you pursue your goals and prove to yourself that you can create change.

Step 15
Step Into Your Future

Let's keep it real: setting intentions isn't just striving for perfection. Life will still throw curveballs and things will still get messy. You will make mistakes, and that's okay. What's different now is you. You've learned to be adaptable. You've learned how to regain control instead of letting things get worse.

1. Letting go of the past creates space in your heart and soul.
2. This relieves stress and makes you feel lighter.
3. Start creating new experiences that bring joy and fulfillment.
4. You will feel alive in ways you've never experienced before.

Honor your new future self in new ways today, not in the future.

1. Plan something fun for yourself; find a new hobby or develop a new skill.
2. Practice self-care and get in the habit of regularly strengthening your mind, body, and soul.
3. Ponder and write the different ways your new mindset has changed your life.

More About Step Into Your Future

Pity parties are no longer your go-to, because you've outgrown that version of yourself. You've grown, and now you know how to keep moving forward with tact, even when life doesn't go as planned. Remember what you have learned.

- You know how to reflect on situations.
- You can process your emotions.
- You have a plan for triggers.
- You can feel your feelings.
- You decide how to act from here on.
- You're applying new habits.
- You're nurturing your body and mind.
- You use music as a mood booster.
- You redecorated your space.
- You cleared out the mental mess.
- You choose faith over fear.
- You have a new set of tools to use.

Congratulations once again, you did it! You have moved through the 15 steps to leave the past and step into your future. You have ended the pity party!

On my website are many resources to help ease you through every phase of your pity party. You can download them all here:
https://endpitypartybook.com

Know this: You are worthy and you matter!

You've finished. Before you go…

Post/Share that you finished this book.

Please star rate this book.

Reviews are solid gold to writers. Please take a few minutes to give us some itty bitty feedback.

ABOUT THE AUTHOR

Keri A. Bentsen believes every party has its time, and when self-pity is the theme, it's time to call it a night. She helps people leave the kind of party that drains you. As a Wellness Life Coach who faced her own setbacks, Keri helps people stop spiraling and start standing in their self-worth.

Her holistic take on healing blends mindset shifts, real-life skills, and a generous scoop of self-compassion. Sometimes the best way forward is to face the facts and then decide to choose something better for yourself. You don't have to stay stuck in the hard stuff; you're allowed to grow through it and rise.

Keri is also a passionate speaker and self-worth advocate on a mission to help people stop settling and start believing they're worthy of more. Through her workshops, talks, and one-on-one support, she works to erase the quiet epidemic of low self-worth, so individuals can finally live the lives they were meant for, with communities that thrive.

Check out Keri's resources on her website for more tips to help ease you through every phase of your pity party. You can check them out here: https://endpitypartybook.com

Wherever you are on your journey, Keri is cheering you on! You've got what it takes to move forward with grace. The pity party is over; now it's your time to shine!

If you enjoyed this Itty Bitty™ book,
you might also like...

- **Your Amazing Itty Bitty™ Power of Living a Purpose-filled Life Book -** Gigi Santiago, MS, AP

- **Your Amazing Itty Bitty™ Magic Mind Book -** Jenny Harkleroad

- **Your Amazing Itty Bitty™ Holistic Experts Compilation Book** - Various Authors

Or any of the many Amazing Itty Bitty™ books available online at www.ittybittypublishing.com

www.ingramcontent.com/pod-product-compliance
Lightning Source LLC
Chambersburg PA
CBHW061305040426
42444CB00010B/2534